Pebble® Plus

Under the Sea
Penguins

by Deborah Nuzzolo

Consulting Editor: Gail Saunders-Smith, PhD

Consultant: Ray Davis
Senior Vice President, Zoological Operations
Georgia Aquarium

Capstone
press®

Mankato, Minnesota

Pebble Plus is published by Capstone Press,
151 Good Counsel Drive, P.O. Box 669, Mankato, Minnesota 56002.
www.capstonepress.com

1 2 3 4 5 6 12 11 10 09 08 07

Library of Congress Cataloging-in-Publication Data
Nuzzolo, Deborah.
    Penguins / by Deborah Nuzzolo.
    p. cm.—(Pebble plus. Under the sea)
    Summary: "Simple text and photographs describe penguins, their body parts, and what
they do"—Provided by publisher.
    Includes bibliographical references and index.
    ISBN-13: 978-1-4296-0033-0 (hardcover)
    ISBN-10: 1-4296-0033-0 (hardcover)
    1. Penguins—Juvenile literature. I. Title. II. Series.
QL696.S473N89 2008
598.47—dc22   2006101928

Editorial Credits
Mari Schuh, editor; Juliette Peters, set designer; Kim Brown, designer; Charlene Deyle, photo researcher

Photo Credits
Bruce Coleman Inc./John Shaw
Corbis/Tim Davis, 4–5, 21
Minden Pictures/Ingo Arndt, 16–17; NPL/Doug Allen, 14–15; NPL/Staffan Widstrand, 6–7; Tui De Roy, 13
Peter Arnold, Inc./Fritz Polking, 18–19; Gerard Lacz, 8–9
Shutterstock/dwphotos, 1; Nik Niklz, 10–11

Note to Parents and Teachers

The Under the Sea set supports national science standards related to the diversity
and unity of life. This book describes and illustrates penguins. The images support
early readers in understanding the text. The repetition of words and phrases helps early
readers learn new words. This book also introduces early readers to subject-specific
vocabulary words, which are defined in the Glossary section. Early readers may need
assistance to read some words and to use the Table of Contents, Glossary, Read More,
Internet Sites, and Index sections of the book.

Table of Contents

What Are Penguins?

Penguins are
black and white birds.
Penguins can swim,
but they can't fly.

Some penguins are
as small as a backpack.
Others are as tall
as three backpacks
stacked end on end.

Body Parts

Penguins flap their flippers
to swim and dive.

Short, stiff feathers
and blubber
keep penguins warm.

11

Penguins use
their sharp beaks
to clean their feathers.

13

What Penguins Do

Penguins dive

to find food.

They catch small fish

and krill with their beaks.

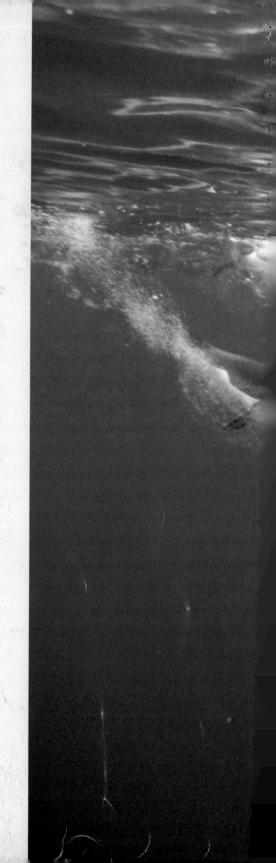

Penguins waddle
and hop on land.
They also slide
on their bellies.

Some penguins build nests
from pebbles and plants.
They lay one or two eggs
each year.

Under the Sea

Penguins spend
most of their lives
swimming under the sea.

Glossary

beak—the hard, pointed part of an animal's mouth

bird—an animal that has feathers, wings and a beak; penguin wings are flippers.

blubber—a layer of fat under a penguin's skin; blubber helps penguins stay warm.

dive—to swim down toward the bottom of a lake or ocean

feathers—a light, fluffy body part that covers a bird's body

flipper—a winglike body part on a penguin

krill—a tiny ocean animal that is similar to shrimp

nest—a place where birds lay their eggs

stiff—not easily bent

waddle—to sway back and forth while walking

Read More

Arnold, Caroline. *A Penguin's World.* Caroline Arnold's Animals. Minneapolis: Picture Window Books, 2006.

Swanson, Diane. *Penguins.* Welcome to the World of Animals. Milwaukee: Gareth Stevens, 2004.

Townsend, Emily Rose. *Penguins.* Polar Animals. Mankato, Minn.: Pebble Books, 2004.

Internet Sites

FactHound offers a safe, fun way to find Internet sites related to this book. All of the sites on FactHound have been researched by our staff.

Here's how:

1. Visit *www.facthound.com*

2. Choose your grade level.

3. Type in this book ID **1429600330** for age-appropriate sites. You may also browse subjects by clicking on letters, or by clicking on pictures and words.

4. Click on the **Fetch It** button.

FactHound will fetch the best sites for you!

Index

Word Count: 109
Grade: 1
Early-Intervention Level: 14